108

15. 00

SLINGSHOTS

(A HIP-HOP POETICA)

KEVIN COVAL

EM PRESS
24041 S. Navajo Dr.
Channahon, IL 60410
www.em-press.com

PROPS FOR SLINGSHOTS...

"Chicago poet Coval, an HBO Def Poet, grapples with questions of identity and compassion. He writes of "latchkeys" marooned in front the television at home and menaced by violence at school. Assessing his own Jewish heritage in "Pieces of Shalom," he wants to "turn my mind on the divine/ without historical frustration." Vehemently condemning hypocrisy, Coval echoes Allen Ginsberg in his spiritual revolt, cosmic vision, and longing for multicultural transcendence. In boldly beautiful and outspoken hip-hop manifestos, he forges links among "all Diaspora people," citing "Dick Gregory and Lenny Bruce," picturing Jack Robinson breaking the color line on the first night of Passover in 1947, and recognizing that davening worshippers in a synagogue are experiencing the same "energy and ecstasy" he experiences when enthralled by hip-hop. Potent metaphors, muscular turns of phrase, a keen political conscience, and a Studs Terkelesque openness to humankind's countless stories fuel Coval's percussive calls for compassion and connection. Accompanied by a CD and graced with cover art by the incomparable Tony Fitzpatrick, this is one potent and positive debut. "

~Donna Seaman, American Library Association, Booklist.

MORE PROPS FOR SLINGSHOTS...

"[Coval] wholeheartedly embraces hip-hop ethics and applies them to every situation, demanding authenticity, questioning authority, and interrogating power structures. Coval's greatest strength is his rhythmic, beautiful prose, but he's relatable-and likeable- for his remarkable honesty and boyish romanticism, his studied understanding of race and class, his unflinching faith in hip-hop culture and over-earnest devotion to heros like KRS-ONE and his willingness to speak truth to power, no matter what the personal cost."

~URB magazine

"*Slingshots* is a visionary spoken word collection guided by an acute sense of spiritual freedom and personal conviction. The inner and outer worlds of politics, hip-hop and love merge to the point of combustion. Kevin Coval is a true verbal assassin and his voice should be used as a weapon for change."

~*Willie Perdomo*
Author of Where a Nickel Costs a Dime *and* Smoking Lovely

"[Coval has] masterfully taken black life and Jewish life, urban life and suburban life, hip-hop and rest of the world and put all these elements together in a cultural gumbo that is quite tasty. A brilliant mind!"

~Chicago Public Radio

"A tour de force ... the whole book is love songs of one kind or another ... He takes on the issues of urban living with a clear, cold eye and with compassion for those left in its wake. The music of Coval's words comes through loud and clear."

~*Rick Massimo,* The Providence Journal

"[*Slingshots*] is divided into four sections. The first... paints a portrait of a quietly tortured suburban existence exacerbated by the slow, steady encroachment of class issues. Coval plops the reader into the center of middle class tragedy. Coval's microscopic lens (then) zooms in on the burgeoning Chicago underground. The poems are wide-eyed and ecstatic. He makes epic warfare of emcee battles, confesses love for a b-girl and carves a path through Chicago landmarks. The poems serve as record of both the personal and communal experience. The final two chapters chronicle Coval's political maturation. It's clear that [he] has learned to focus hip-hop's mistrust of authority, questioning the hierarchy within his own community."

~Time Out Chicago

"...stuttering staccato lines breaking against what follows, internal rhymes tripping through the verse like dominoes. A verse that demands to be chanted. This is communion for the crowd; it's as if Coval is narrating their life."

~Chicago Reader

"[Coval] familiarizes himself with numerous dialects... and mixes them in with Yiddish/Hebrew words and descriptions of ancient Jewish tradition that creates an art so honest it would have emcee Matisyahu lamenting his lack of creativity."

~The Emory Wheel

"Kevin Coval's work is like the dirt bike racers of poetry. It moves, it sways, it dips, and sometimes flips ... A powerful collection by a powerful voice that matters."

~Luis J. Rodriguez
Award-winning poet & poetry publisher;
Author of My Nature is Hunger

"Kevin Coval's debut book is fresh! High art... at times it's incendiary and at others, personal and compelling. His poems feel urgent."

~Elemental Magazine

"*Slingshots* is like a midnight craps game between Studs Terkel, Gwendolyn Brooks and Big Daddy Kane, thrown against a synagogue wall. Kevin Coval's wordplay is fierce, frenetic and funny, but these words didn't come to play. This is poetry as community dialogue, poetry as distilled-essence-of-rhyme-cipher, poetry that scours both the world and the self for stones big enough to fling at the Goliaths of our times."

~Adam Mansbach
Author of Angry Black White Boy, or
The Miscegenation of Macon Detornay

PROPS FOR KEVIN COVAL...

"This is one of my favorite poets."
~Mos Def

"Voice of the new Chicago... brilliant, funny, magnificent and intensely personal... should stand up there with the work of Carl Sandburg, and I don't say that lightly."
~Rick Kogan, WGN

"...raw, straight, no chaser. That's the real lethal weapon right there."
~Michael Eric Dyson

"...important, maybe even essential words to live by." ~Chicago Tribune Magazine

"In his work Coval has shown a celebration of the working man — of the underdogs."
~The Daily Herald

"Kevin Coval wields the spoken word and his brilliant social imaginings into irresistible invitations to build a better world. His passion to dismantle artificial barriers and help people work together holds promise both tender and fiery."

~Kathy Kelly
2003 Nobel Peace Prize Nominee; Author
of Other Lands Have Dreams: From
Baghdad to Pekin Prison; Co-founder of
Voices in the Wilderness

EM Press
24041 S. Navajo Dr.
Channahon, IL 60410
www.em-press.com

SLINGSHOTS: A HIP-HOP POETICA (book/CD)
© 2005 by Kevin Coval. All rights reserved.

Cover art, "Chicago Sky #4" by Tony Fitzpatrick

*Book design, typeset, CD design by Emily Evans for naïveté studios
(www.naivetestudios.org)*

Cover design by Gregory Harms

ISBN: 0-9708012-4-6

Printed in the United States of America by Rochelle Printing
for EM Press, LLC.

Second Printing, 2006

for Stephen,
we share blood and fire,
i poet in the footsteps
of your path

&

for Joyce,
who holds our family
and communities together,
tikkun olam, example in the flesh

&

for my mom,
my backbone,
i am awed by your strength-
you taught me to stand up

&

for my pops,
you are the greatest
storyteller in the world,
the kindest man i know

when you feel within that your mind is very, very warm from combining the letters and that through the combinations you understand new things that you have not attained by human tradition nor discovered on your own through mental reflection, then you are ready to receive the abundant flow, and the abundance flows upon you, arousing you again and again.

~Abraham Abulafia
13th Century Jewish Mystic

...but by men of strange lips and with an alien tongue, YHWH will speak to this people...

~Isaiah 28:11

maybe i should write some songs like mozart cuz many people don't believe rap is an art

~KRS-ONE

CONTENTS ▪ ▪ ▪ ▪ ▪ ▪ ▪ ▪ ▪ ▪ ▪ ▪

Foreword by Bill Ayers, author of *Fugitive Days*; Distinguished Professor of Education, University of Illinois-Chicago

Introduction by Jeff Chang, American Book Award Winner, 2005, *Can't Stop Won't Stop: A History of the Hip-Hop Generation*

pieces of shalom

shell toes and a pocket full of verses

letters before buffing

slingshots

...this is a book on identity,

on shifting alliances and

allegiances, of trying to

live a moral life in a world

gone mad, of politics, yes,

and borders and boundaries

and memory and dreams

and cages and holes and

journeys...

~Bill Ayers

FOREWORD

The Chicago poet Gwendolyn Brooks opened her piece on the dedication of the giant Picasso sculpture in the center of downtown with a question: "Does man love Art?" Her answer: "Man visits Art, but squirms/Art hurts. Art urges voyages." So true, so true.

And here comes Kevin Coval, in the tradition—like Brooks a Chicago poet, both a dazzling artist and a committed, hardworking teacher, a writer who draws inspiration and energy from the people he encounters in the neighborhoods, around the corner, someone who feels the boom-boom-boom of daily life, and reimagines through the rhythm of the street.

Like Brooks, his art "urges voyages."

Coval claims that "hip-hop asks one eternal question/what do you represent?" These poems are an extended reflection and a kind of answer—this is a book on identity, on shifting alliances and allegiances, of trying to live a moral life in a world gone mad, of politics, yes, and borders and boundaries and memory and dreams and cages and holes and journeys both imposed and chosen. This book invites a step outside the safety of "home" into a wider world called "exile"—exile's vocation is hope, its direction, possibility. Uprooted, unhinged, Coval discovers in crossing over "the bridge of whiteness" the possibility of deracination, of real human solidarity and, just perhaps, the possibility of pathways to our collective survival. Coval sings of the possibility of love of all kinds: paternal, maternal, fraternal, spiritual, carnal, platonic, fleeting and eternal, healing and searing. Coval sees what's available and he "makes it weird," makes it new, makes it hopeful.

It's about the beat, too—the sound and the rhythm that carries the hope. It's about a sense of dislocation, but it's the displacement of a pilgrim not the cynic. Coval claims an all-encompassing diaspora as home, all those souls singing their various freedom dreams—"we speak in tongues," he says, in different idioms, each negotiation, every translation, dynamic, idiosyncratic, complex. We feel the multiple perspectives and the double-consciousnesses of DuBois, the fugitive invisibility of Ellison—"beneath the radar screen/ of dominant linguistics" Coval says. Together, the teachers, the poets, the elders and the youth are "crying our culture back to life."

Kevin Coval speaks with a singular voice from a new generation suffering the age-old question: Who in the world am I? Who am I in the world? Where will I find and take my place? And what will I make of all that I've been made? Coval joins artists ancient and contemporary as he dives into the wreckage, swims toward a shore called life. This is a book to stuff into your back pocket, nourishment for the struggle to live free and enlightened, or to squirrel away in your backpack next to the vitamin C, the bandana, the spray paint and the Vaseline, fragments for survival. Coval looks uneasily at the world he's inherited, he links arms with his students and his fellow artists. His mind is cocked, his pen is locked and loaded, his words, louder than a bomb.

Bill Ayers, author of Fugitive Days
Distinguished Professor of Education, University of Illinois-Chicago
Chicago, 2004

Although hip-hop projects

itself as aggressive sport,

it is at its most truthful as

the unmuzzled cry of the

silenced, the fragile, and the

unprotected, as the rock in

the slingshot.

~Jeff Chang

INTRODUCTION

Like James Brown's funk, Kevin Coval's poetry starts on The One, or as KRS-One put it, "Poetry, you know it's me," part bold assertion and part surgical dissection of self. Forming identity is an equally creative and destructive force. Hip-hop cuts close even as it liberates.

Coval was raised in the white Chicago suburbs like a fish out of water. About the time that Billy "Upski" Wimsatt's "Bomb The Suburbs," another young Chicagoan's hip-hop manifesto, hit the streets, Coval was electrified by a one-time generational shockwave. At the famously departed Afrocentric shop and café in Wicker Park known as Lit X, hip-hop gave him the words to begin seeking without knowing what he would find.

He examined a childhood churned by white-collar fears of falling, drug-fueled escapism, separation, and suicidal tendencies, and deconstructed his Jewishness as if he were trying to find his own current in the flow of histories, personal and epic. Hip-hop had promised, in Afrika Bambaataa's words, peace, love, unity, and having fun. But it also offered much more. From Bob Marley's One Love to KRS's Poetry, hip-hop's primary motion was toward wholeness—the suburbs toward the city, white toward Black, Israeli toward Palestinian—the end of -isms and schisms. So "Slingshots" charts Coval's roots journey to a worldview.

He returns to the city and the struggle, and looks to build back community from the block up. The city's gentrification is not about the increasing valuation of buildings, but the decreasing valuation of interconnected systems of vibrant life. But Coval's is a different kind of New Urbanism, one not predicated on aesthetic nostalgia or brutal individualism or boiler room speculation. He finds a love of place tangible in a vast Studs Terkel cast of characters, from those who shaped the past to those who trade futures to those muddling through the present. He captures the way that they touch each other across race, class, and gender the same way that dominoes fall.

Although hip-hop projects itself as aggressive sport, it is at its most truthful as the unmuzzled cry of the silenced, the fragile, and the unprotected, as the rock in the slingshot. The politics of abandonment and containment created the hip-hop generation. Our aesthetic and our politics must be about empathy and engagement, freedom and commitment.

Coval describes the long rich chain of life and myth that connects William Stafford to his uncle Steven and Luis J. Rodriguez to Jam Master Jay and Emma Goldman to Suheir Hammad and Elijah to Bambaataa and Hashem to Rakim, and all of them to us and to each other. Coval's words reach for reconciliation and redemption, to water the garden and feed the hungry, to spring up from nothing then spin around and drop down, right on The One. They pull up the people and shake down the powerful. In the end, they come 360 degrees right back home.

Jeff Chang
American Book Award Winner, 2005, Can't Stop Won't Stop: A History of the Hip-Hop Generation
September 2005

pieces of shalom

pieces of shalom

in mother's womb we wept
quiet not quite aware of anxiety
around father's face clenched like fist
fearing when he'd have to be
clocking in to work

capitalism sucked
his life force bank
broke it in the arms
of alcohol and other women

it gave mother ulcers
before she snorted early eighties
deception, the same cosmetic smile
her white mother picket-fenced
around the defense of her husband
cracked like eyes in the skull of a lunatic
she wild slipped depression dreams narcotic
tranquil lies filled her afternoons
glass ceilings tore her skin and nancy reagan
just said no   to families

we latchkeys
sat morning long in front of walt disney
hard-core gangster corporate reality raps
pounding, as our parents punched each other
in toys 'r us aisles searching for a way to say
                              i love you

our fathers fought themselves in Vietnam
brought the war back in body bags like the CIA
did heroin / nightly shooting up
violence in the bedroom

we are told   to be cool
                 to be popular
                 to search for gold
                 of starting salary

but at recess we regret
turn angst inward, stand
in front of mirror with shotgun
unsure of where to point
           when to pull

my brother drank drano at thirteen
Jessica swallowed diet pills i remember
my mother hysterically hugging her sons in the hallway asking
           why are the children killing themselves?
                                         and i don't know

Hebrew
but did learn
hip-hop

in my reality / all this wackness i couldn't handle see / wanted to squash this situation turn my
mind on the divine / without historical frustration / i sought my generation / hip-hop kids breakin
down nouns and verbs to relate reality mystically / inclusivity / based on skills and never skin / i
(re)present creation / from my light within / cuz how you gonna build apocalyptic space stations
and tell me about sin / i'd rather dwell near Ayin / from nothingness we do begin / g-dSelf forth
could only manifest within

i told my rabbi whose angry hands hit me
i wasn't a goodman or freidman or rosenberg
but Abraham crashing idols in my father's corner store

he said i'd be nobody
i told him there was no/body
to be

he said *jews are the chosen people, we have a covenant with G-d*
i said *fuck you* / stripped to show him naked
i'd stitched hymen and foreskin of human to my skin
told him *we'll recreate the covenant*
                            make it weird
we'll all come running out our homes collecting memories
of buttafly indigenous peoples (break) dancing to severe imperialism
throw our bodies on black earth / link pinky toes / belly rings / dreadlocks / *pe'at*

mad headz on each others' stomach laughing / until our hope seeps into seed
grows sustainable institutions / sacred sites we won't have to wail at
walls for murdered masses but erect Meccas of secret sectors marked graffiti
bombs in the minds of Latino Picassos

we'll know whereabouts thru walkabouts
rapping rhythms griots spit in the gutter
maps to guide us if we fall

                                                              off course

i am beginning
chopping this corroded shell of self
until i see eternity in the death of my skin

in morning
i sit in the early of nothingness

at lunch i meet wind by the lake
we feed each other strawberries

after classes my crew circles in ciphers
flex lyrical acrobatics like Sufis swirling ecstatic

i walk homeless streets passing invisible shaman sessions
home where i wrap my body in *tallis* and write out of my mind

                                                              into Hashem

we are beginning
these sons and daughters
who weren't down enough
for the economic trickle

these sisters and brothers
who grew up chained in one bedroom fatherless homes
saw the american ideal paraded before them every waking moment
one day realized it could never be their dream but was dependent
upon the perpetuation of their sleeping nightmares

these kids in the cities
these kids in the suburbs
who found salvation one night tripping or rolling or blowed
listening to KRS-ONE listening to Jimi Hendrix listening
to Brian Culhane describe the immensity of the universe
and w/ each phrase or riff or verse flip change into eternity

this family
whose obsessive-compulsive disorder dictates our yoga practice
whose nervous fidgets count breaths between wooden beads and breakbeats
whose manic depression is balancing on the needles of turntables
      in the pages of infinite journals
whose stuttering *ah's* gather nightly
      screaming into open microphones
      meditative   *olam habah*

what norman rockwell didn't capture

on soccer field moms
blue chips off the old stock option
orange slice crescents into the pond
of their mothers' faces empty like stomachs
beneath searchlight gossip and broken seashells

they are practicing for the MCATs
have run out of frogs and pig fetus
bang chests like orangutans caged
in the basement behind donkey kong

near keebler elf slave quarters
Ari and Rachel consume tvs
for dinner cut washing machine detergent
with popsicle sticks and slurpee
psychotropes through nights of insomnia

their father is a long way from work
crunching numbers and bodies of color
in the parlors of monetary madams

he entertains other lives
with bleu cheese olive martinis
in a cul-de-sac not his own

he sleeps with the enigma
who whispers american dreams
from the balcony of his one night stand

in the bedroom castle we are
barred in all the king's pleasures:
sex sockets surround a floor of plug-ins
Barbie in a barbed-wire push-up bra
GI Joe bathes in a circus of pin ups
and shell casings

the last time we sat in the dining room
Uncle Dave stuck a bread knife thru his abdomen
his blood is covered by a throw rug and the silent
conversations we don't have

social science experiment summer hoops camp
                                    roommates
we shared toothpaste and pillows, fighting stories
neighborhoods, father fists, cocaine line crossed cousins

awake after hours hall monitors sleep, us boys
new to pubic hair and deepened voices, wrestle
in awkward bodies finding the retardations
of racial understanding

    your mama so black, she the pin-up girl for the Ku Klux Klan
    your mama's a redneck, skin rare out that Nazi oven too early

Dick Gregory and Lenny Bruce
trading jabs over gatorade, giggling
nervous like girls who see their father
naked for the first time

    Black from the city
    i heard white lies about
    the Green he lived on
    bass waves and break beats
    in the last ditch efforts of integration
    before he was wiped out of city landscapes
    with post-industrial red, white and blue prints

check this out, he said
from across the room
and frisbeed BDP's
By All Means Necessary
with KRS on the cover
holding uzi like Malcolm
peering out a window to reality
i'd been brained blind not to see
                                    Jamal dropped dime on me
back flat in the dorm bunk
across the room, brand new jordans
and a ball he'd hold like a teddy bear
when dreaming and shoot the sky awake

arm straight as a tree trunk
hand still like a swan's face

7

what moms had to do for a michael jordan autographed shoe

she didn't want to but we were like cheerleaders
whining until victory, how could she not at least try
one date with a Chicago Bull's assistant coach

he picked her up in the summertime off-season
mom made him wait with Eric and I in the backyard
on faux chez lounges we stole from the alley of ace hardware
she powdered her self pretty upstairs, anesthetizing for the evening

he looked old, much older than he did on tv
more like a grandfather, skin beginning to leather and spot
purple veins like rivers in his huge hands, a championship
pinky ring, gray hair greased back, capped teeth, he smelled
like menthol and pomade, wore a dark suit like the movie
gangsters, told us about his professional playing days, we yawned
bursting in anticipation of when we could ask for stories about mike

mom made cheese roll-ups
white bread + butter, american cheese
rolled, toasted, held together by tooth picks
our favorite appetizer, she served
herself the usual 5 o'clock martini at 4

                                                            hit 3

                            by 7

it was warm outside
sweat built on the coach's brow
doubled teamed with questions
he batted at like tipped passes
looked at his rolex, sensing desperation
Eric and I put the press on, *do you think*
you could get us a Michael Jordan autograph
pleeeeeeeeeeeeeeeeeeaseeeeeee?????????

mom broke her gait toward the sliding door
back stiffened, braced for the answer, he paused
gazed at my mom entering her rented townhome
like a slow-motion replay he turned toward us
said *let me see what i could get my hands on*

tradition[1]

hine matov
folk song my father's favorite
legacies i wrestle with

----

1 *hai coups are a variation on the traditional Japanese form, haiku, which has seventeen syllables. hai coups have eighteen syllables, for the Hebrew letter* hai, *which means life. hai coups point towards a self-mastery and/or radical life change, as in coup d' etat. there are seven in this collection to signify the days of creation seven meaning perhaps the realm of infinity, where we rest and seek to inhabit the sacred.*

stealing home

please america do not write your history books grinning
branch rickey's false generosity / he and major league baseball
murdered Josh Gibson / left him drunk / waiting for Joe DiMaggio to say hello

please know slavery and the color line ended
cuz economics not ethics / Blacks in the big league / a marketing strategy
a bobblehead doll at the door for the first 20,000

April 15, 1947 was the first night of Passover
as well as opening day and the Dodgers wear white and blue at home
Ebbets Field, Brooklyn / where 26,623 witnessed Moses point towards Jerusalem
with a Louisville Slugger / cross white chalk lines that marked what was foul

and the youngest sons and daughters of america asked
why is this night different

this night
when my family remembers Exodus
with bitter herbs diced apples walnuts cinnamon
to symbolize mortar of the pyramids

this night
lathering our front door with lamb's blood
to notify the Angel of Death we are working here
each generation revealing new freedoms

this night
when a black man became a hero to my blond headed father
and took a whole people on his back to move them across a sea

Jack Robinson
you made our pitchers balk   with outrageous leadoffs
every eye in every stadium on you / gasping for breath / crouched

                                                      in ready
                                                      position

able to turn four balls   into a triple
the Negro league in an army-issued duffel sack / Cool Papa Bell beneath your cap
you poured a fifty-year old gumbo onto the precious gem of a national pastime
with spices and speed / our palate desired and detested your grace and ease

your majesty floating between white bags

our jealousy scribbled death threats / booed epitaphs
shouted our sickness from grandstands and bleachers
belching the mustard aftertaste of white supremacy
                                                        crackers, Jack
in the peanut gallows of ethnocentrism
plotting strategies to overthrow your dominance

              and we've yet to leave your sons alone
              in the streets our heads flinch over shaky shoulders
              keep an eye on their quick feet / for they are all stealing
              home and our catcher will not hesitate to gun them down

Papa came home on The Sabbath

Mama Ellie's yellow kitchen, her hands
circle two flames three times before she
covered her eyes to pray for the world

each friday at sundown we'd rip challah
pass torn egg twists; hand to cousin's hand
to mother's mouth, i thought it yiddish
                              cholly days

after the work week, the men tired
beat from sales trips thru midwest
small town michigan indiana routes
Papa Sy returned back worn, knotted
like his temper, but home

                              we'd wait for him
in the living room Adam, Jill, brother Eric
playing *J-J-J-Jam On It* on the home stereo
poplocking arms- waves between our bodies
when the garage door cracked, tape ejected
fearing what would happen if Papa heard
bass resonating in the corners of his home

he'd walk thru the door like achilles
returning from war with treasures:
key chains, candy, postcard pictures
of waterfalls, forests and the elegant
bottle that he said held G-d's syrup

he'd gather us in his arms
sit each child on his lap and pour
mogen david into the kiddush cup
his father rushed out of germany
he'd sing the *brucha* whispering
l'chaim into our soft ears
a sip for each grandchild
his big paw holding the silver goblet
our hands around his like *tiffilin*
close to our heart, close to our mind

opening the door for Elijah

in sunday school
i made our *seder* plate
drew simple pictures of food
we ate *Pesach* night as symbol

zeroa, the lamb bone Abraham struck in place of Issac
beitza, an egg boiled round to encompass life and death
maror, bitterness to burn our eyes as in egypt
charoset, chopped apples, nuts, wine and cinnamon
mortar our ancestors laid for pharaoh's pyramids,
karpas, fresh and green dipped twice in salt water
an orange for women on the *bima*
matzah is our sustenance

we could not wait for yeast to rise,
and fled quiet like *Bubbe* Pearl did poland
head wrapped in a babushka of raisins
like David did austria in the rain
of shattered temples / like two brothers
slowed-tongued Moses and Aaron
articulating *Yisrael*

velvet covers the *matzah*, an heirloom
my great-grandmother sewed in russia
before the czar stopped protecting her
from cossacks

at the table i'd flank *Zayde's* left arm
his oldest grandson learning the ritual
meal, our history of resistance; the White
Rose in germany, Goldman in exile
Goodman and Schwerner

Jews
who in the face of an empire
spoke freedom

before the meal concluded and the women wash
Zayde would send me to open the door for Elijah
whose kiddush cup sat in the center of our *seder* table

Elijah
who is the wayward's sheperd
the scribe of every tear in heaven
who we offer the fifth cup of wine
so he will stay and drink with us
because if he stays and drinks
gets drunk and sings, it is said
the messiah will come

i'd hold my breath
turn the knob towards the sun
waiting to see if G-d's prophetic ghost
stood with ram's horn sounding the call
that next year's feast will be in Jerusalem

he was never there
each year we wait still, for Elijah

as a kid, i thought
Bubbe's cooking kept him away

i now think he is a rock
knocking on closed doors
of the knesset with words
the weight of stones

i think he is the tongue of young poets
who scream their bodies to bits
in markets and borders
they are barred from crossing

i am the oldest grandson
struggling to ask my family
on the night of our own bondage

if Elijah stood dark skinned
in the doorway of our grandparents'
split-level suburban home
would we invite him to wash
his hands on our doorstep
fill his belly at our table
would we allow him to rest
after centuries of wandering
or would we bury his memory
with bulldozers

family feud

my mother's voice rises
like defense shields when i ask if she wants
my daughter to be murdered by bombs
built of self-delusion

my father screams
fists thru my face when i mention
this new war aids right wing rhetoric
and maybe the government is involved
in ways known secret books from now

my grandfather gone three years, returns
between john wayne AMC marathons
george m. cohan in front of a dead tv
tells me ike and macarthur are patriots
i should leave this country if i won't
lay truth down for it

my Uncle Steven
thirty years earlier took manuscripts to manhattan
moved office mail and furniture, bike messengered
in the dusk of empire, left wife and german shepard
sister, brother and Mother Ellie, draft dodged and drugged
rather than continue scraping knuckles against his father's
nearsightedness

my family says i remind them of him
every time i open my mouth and dream

hai coup

hip-hop was mother
and father for latchkey kids
busy birthing fresh worlds

breakbeats let my g-dSelf loose

one time i heard Afrika Bambatta say
when you hear the breakbeat / you let your g-dSelf get loose

all my life i knew i was a Jewish neurotic / constantly looking over my shoulder
to see if the neighbors gonna turn cossacks or moors or informants in the mccarthy scare
but i didn't want shit to do with the culture or religion / at 16 i told my best friend
not to call me Jewish / cuz comin up i'd only had negative associations with Judaism
like getting kicked out our synagogue cuz moms owed mad money for Hebrew school
and all these sons of lawyers driving around in holocaust death camp machines
all classist / thinkin they slick cuz they could afford the new jordans / while i gotta work
at a hot dog stand to save up for the payless generic brand / and they couldn't play ball anyway
they'd be listening to the fuckin band genesis but not readin it / i'd get an ear full in sunday
school about justice and our history to see the so-called elders whose community i was gonna
join up at my bar mitzvah being traders / corporate bankers protecting the economic interests
of the ruling class who let us hang out a minute ago for the first time in like...   2000 years
and now we gonna be all glad and american and patriotic and eat white bread on Passover / but
i knew that wasn't me

i couldn't afford a BMW or new clothes at the mall / and didn't want it / comin up
in the 80's all i wanted to do was rock African medallions, some juju beads and hang out
with X-Clan / but i felt like nobody would understand where i was coming from / so i just buried
myself in the music / kept on hearing the refrain / *it ain't where ya from*
its where ya at /re-present re-re-present/ it ain't where ya from its where ya at

hip-hop asks one eternal question / what do you   represent

it was when i was in a Hasidic synagogue in montreal
during Rosh Hashanah and Yom Kippur, the night of Kol Nidre
the most important time on the Jewish calendar
where we have one final evening to be inscribed in the book of life
and pray with all of our might that i saw my people

                                                    head nodding
swaying back and forth   bowing supplicating
bodies   twisting frentic, *tallit* whirling like tendrils, bodies
bearded n sweating   popping   submissive   to the rhythm

                                                        of prayer

for the first time i *davened*
with the energy and ecstasy of a b-boy in battle

Hashem moved the crowd

Master of Cermony
Lord of the Universe

shell toes and a pocket full of verses

freestyle

my room
a cipher
alone
juggling
       words

no where
to be found

elegy for Lit X

i never said shit / nervous to read
my little raps before a kingdom of griots

but i loved the way you smelled

sandalwood sweat cowry shells locked in dreads and wool hats
packed flesh Rastafarian hymns wafting frankincense blunt smoke
bookstore hemp oil weed wisdom saturday night live spot

i met children prostrating with poems in the altar of your womb
legitimate lyricists / street corner scholars / seditious dissonance
on the drums of hip-hop disobedience / a basement
before underground became a commercial calling card

Mama Africa in Wicker Park
you kept it real
                    it was / all good

Lit X like Malcolm in prison
i changed in your lap lullabies

KRS told me to read *How to Eat to Live* by Elijah Muhammad
only your shelves carried the brown paperback / seven years later
i do not consume the devil's diet but feed on fruits and vegetables

Mama i am starving since you were kidnapped
i have not eaten properly since they shot you
with property tax / i cannot sleep at night
without hearing you scream

they are fucking with us, Mama
they built master's metaphor / atop your grave site
expect us to work there / cuz it's the only place we can
get health insurance / they spit and trample on your open tomb

we will not bury you, Mama / you are not dead
only on a vacation we needed / to organize ourselves better
learn more / wrangle wild heads / into the dream of the struggle

we are building Mama
all of us / waiting / on you
to resurrect

monday nights at the blue groove lounge

Jesse de La Pena cuttin
down stairs in the basement
bass hit my chest, underground
head-nodding meditation
ancient forms of repetitive movement
found in buddhist recitations

pressed the pavement
w/ sullied shell toes and a pocket full of verses
tryin find an open mic to open my mind
into a spine that felt my searches

i heard bursts kid
bushels of blasted battle hymns
scribbled into notebooks / warring ourselves
within these pages / acting out on stages
against crooks who been corrupted through the ages
stand naked in front strangers on a regular basis
tryin to find flow and meta-stasis / tryin to tell the stories
behind the kind eyes i'm constantly embraced with

white boy ballad for a southern b-girl
set to A Tribe Called Quest's *Bonita Applebaum*

at the base of the stair case you walk like wind's b-girl
carry crayons and colored chalk / armed to bomb sidewalks
with intricate hopscotch patterns so women with grocery carts
of babies and kids with latch keys in their pockets can play
on their way home

i dig crates to find the joint to serenade you with
wanna drop lines to catch your ear / reel to reel
you in/to recognizing the melody of an old skool jam
take you back like extension cord jump ropes to blocks
hot from shorties playing in opened fire hydrants
not fire opened on playgrounds by drunks high
on short ties to economic stability

                              word
you be mad psychic
knew i'd be down to name each eyelash
curling toward heaven / each lock spinning out your head
like thoughts collaged in disc jock sonic orchestrations

we sit on concrete steps protecting the shore
line city planners didn't plan on us crossing
bragin breaths in divine dozens like brahmin
takin bout each other's mama / collectin
quiz show points for culture's trivia like
what wuz Big Daddy Kane's first album or
who first got up all-city graff tag new york

i think i have more points

but there are things i can't tell you
like what it feels to be black in a white school in a white world in a white car
when the driver turns the radio to the black station cuz they giving you a ride
to the other side of mississippi

Ellison wrote the invisible life you live
in two worlds across tracks with black people
talkingworkinglovingstrugglingmakingnoises
i've only heard on record

you're like a hip-hop song
each note hinting at history / a eulogy
of etymologies i trace grooves with needles to find you
on your grandparents porch in green grass Louisiana
slow day southern music / lemonade cool / a girl
amongst the monks of willows weeping for the fallen
soldiers and suns set too early / in the afternoon

you gotta put me on
the basslines you live by
the funk of maple sap / stuck to your tongue

you gotta put me on
like mardi gras masks so we can parade the streets
where martyers were run down and murdered on
go to their gravestones / hold hands / wonder why
we stand in separate cemeteries

you gotta put me on
so my parents come correct / say they do mind
if i date a black girl with head wrapped round stories
sliced out tongues of mother testimonies

you gotta put me on
to the southern slang indigenous linguistic resistance
you n crew spit at institutions / the swaggering drawl
y'all draw over generations of stoops in Jackson
around dominos and double dutch in Watts
in the juke joint swamps of Zora's Eatonville

you gotta put me on
like those rainbow knee high socks you rock
with that camouflage lid you look ill in

                              can you let me know

                                        right now

pleeeeeeeeeeeeeeeasssssssssssse

fear of a black planet

a side

idris fell in love
when Spike let *fight the power*
open his movie n Rosie Perez
power moved the running man
red boxing gloves, sweat, tight abs
African features

Radio Rahiem became hip-hop
super-hero juiced by 20 D energizers
he boom boxed duality w/ 2 four-fingered rings
walked the hood in hightops with a hightop fade
carryin a portable block party

b side

the record used to hang behind the counter
at Reckless on North Milwaukee, a black
moon above the huddle of indie rock kids'
shoulders / taking their time to ring you up

krista got it for idris
cuz he wuz real / good to her
last week when it wuz cold

he drew a warm water footbath
picked her up from work in a taxi
got groceries, cleaned his apartment
let her sleep when he woke to write
rhymes for his next solo joint

first edition got lyrics in the jacket
back when hip-hop thought
it could save us

idris said he's gonna
knock krista up now   & get/ta
populatin the planet

          they fear

rasin hell

around the house i'd stalk carpeted rooms like a b-boy
with cerebal palsy, clumsy with a fake bop step and dip
reciting the last track on RUN DMC's second record

i'm proud to be black y'all and that's a fact y'all
and if ya try to what's mine I take it back y'all
it's like that-(ditdit-dit ditdit dit- likylikyliky)

Harriet Tubman, Malcolm X, Ali, Jesse Owens
absent from the white pages of history, were here
in my bedroom, out the mouths of Kings from Queens
secrets my teachers didn't know i armed myself with

when moms told me to look in the mirror
                                                    i did

while i was supposed to be memorizing wars
learning stock markets, trading baseball cards
planning my funeral

The Day Jam Master Jay Died

woke unsure how to pay rent
check hadn't come in from county
too many months living like artist
with no net to break the fall

went to my brother's class at Kelvyn Park
taught Luis Rodriguez in freshman honors
two poems about neighborhood folk / one
heroin-addicted guitar player and the other
man angry in Humboldt Park killing a car

gave a reading at Wright College
theater full of aging teens and faculty
after the set this skinny white kid comes over
gives me props for a poem about graff writers
i ask if he writes, *ELOTES* he says
no shit i say *i've been digging you*
for years over red and brown line tracks
first seen you up on that truck at Chicago
and Halsted / *that's me* he said

ate with Eboo downtown near Loyola
he lectures to a class of grad students
about discovery and inheritance / he is brilliant
in describing our engagement with modernity
we encounter the vastness of cultural practice
and build bridges back home he says

i think of Isabel / young writer at Kelvyn Park
Bindi between her eyebrows / picture of Lady Guadalupe
in her notebook / she reads the Bhagavad Gita in Spanish
with her Aunt who teaches Yoga at the Church
and i tell this class my path back to Judaism
was paved in breakbeats

walk to the train
get home / call my girl
she lives in Brooklyn
on my bed / she tells me

Jam Master Jay was shot
his head spilled onto the control panels
of his studio in Queens

it's fucked up she said
it's fucked up i said

said we'd talk tomorrow
hung up and my apartment was silent
like there was no music in my apartment
my apartment was silent like my childhood
memories silenced tonight like the music

-eulogy-

Chuck D said John Lennon was killed today
and i miss Pac and Big more than ever
i am Holden Caulfield watching hope break in the stalls of public bathrooms
i am Pete Rock and C.L. Smooth reminiscing over the fallen body of b-boy
Trouble T-Roy and dying hip-hop birth sites falling wayside to the pounding beats
of green-fisted real estate agents and the hard crack rock drug wars american wages
on her children creating culture with turntables

we have been here before

and i want Scott La Rock back to break up all this violence
i want Big L to throw a peace sign up in the air and DREAM
and Ramon and all the other graffiti artists killed in the line of their calling
to come back and bomb the World Trade Center
with the biggest streaked wildstyles the sky has ever seen:
a mural for the forgotten spray painted on the clouds
a gold chain cast across the sun
a single shell toe held up in the air

it was Jam Master Jay who introduced me to the culture
who soothed me over the bridge of whiteness and rock
it was his cool lean arms wrapped around chest / head back
in black fedora / no laces in his adidas / he stole electricity
to light the block parties / reparations / for all the stars exploded
before he could play the last song they requested / he'd send shine
beams on vinyl / into the distant homes of the sun starved
and let us bask in his light scratching scarce sounds / found
digging the landfills / of america's sonic consciousness

                                          it's not bad meaning bad but bad meaning
                                          it's not bad meaning
                                          it's not bad meaning
                                          it's not

elements

sun bombs morning
train, passengers
awake in a gallery
of sky, aerosol
streaks toward night
in ocean layups, fresh burners
bless day's new skin

water builds with moon
over base wave lines
spits rain on all headz
splits crust's stiff pores
open tongued lexicons
get loose, flow on&on
anything insight

earth keeps time
cuts continents
consciousness breaks
between scratched surfaces
alters samples like traffic
stampede or water gurgle
cre-ates deep as canyons

wind is middle passage
transport S. Bronx pop-locks
to S. Africa, sails seven generations
bringing noise to be girls and be boys
that be recycling spheres, helicopters
atmospheric gymnastic kung-fu capoiera
patterns not fronts

again & again & again

nothing fight (a battle cry)
for hip-hop/as who deserve the nobel peace prize

the spot is hot

headz sport ski goggles / coats puff like egos
camouflage crews in tim boots / chew ginseng roots
b-girls smell like Egypt / skin smoothed by shea butter

everyone is too broke to bling

nag champa burns like apartments / this loft
once housed machinery parts parents lost jobs to
abandoned it holds the thumping heart of their children
who tonight reek of innovation

plywood on cinder blocks elevate a stage
speakers rattle bass lines atop trashcans
like 2 kids on a bicycle

turntables wobble but won't fall down
DJ Cutout handles vinyl like dough
flings breaks at the crowd spreading electro funk
over South African boot stomp droppin classics
that send congregants skyward to night's peak

the call is made by Ank-1 / would-be-*chazzan*
younger brother of Cutout *peace the mic's open*
we gettin to ready battle / y'all havin a good time

the crowd leaves him hangin like half a high five

Cutout lowers the volume so his brother can shine
yo C, i don't think they heard, if y'all love hip-hop
make some noise Ank ropes headz like he got a lasso
wranglin the crowd's focus from b-boy acrobatics
to *scream if ya wit me and ya knowhatimean*
somebody / anybody / everybody / screeeeam...

MC Prolific is the first to kick ballistics
this lanky light skinned linguistic literati
spits lyric to slash fake freestyle word
written rhymes murders wack emcees
with wit and tightly packed punch lines

droppin more dimes than corner spots
when cops round and lookouts yell *one time*

Sansei spits second
grabs the mic like a samurai
shoulders squared, left arm a rigid angle
before his face, he bombs kids mentals
like Pearl Harbor leavin swollen red suns
tattooed to listeners lips like languages stolen
forgotten, recrafted in undetainable tongues

Medusa throws hexes to get fresh wit
around the necks of men who set trip
they get ripped when she wrecks ship
all over the deck swabs headz with
styles that drop drip like water flow
mimic moon pulls peers in undertow
cycles feminine rippin the mic menstrual

the next to flex is Profound
from the top of the dome the microphone
gets blessed with the holy angst of Allah
medium of Moses and Malcolm X
he protests flows nonindigenous
forces nay sayers to say yes
yes y'all and it don't stop

the crowd joins his chorus
yes yes y'all and it don't stop
he rides the shoulders of waves
yes yes y'all and it don't stop
                    and it don't stop
                    and it don't stop
                    and it don't stop
                    and it don't stop
                    and it don't stop
                    and it don't stop
                    and it don't stop

plea for the wack emcee

please!
please!
please!   stop

            stop   frontin
            stop   hustlin
            stop   mimickin

imperialist minstrels that only leave you hunted
players get played by bigger players like your mama in the dozens
            hesaidshesaidhesaidshesaidshewasn't   talk
oblivious to our function: uplift n unite like we wuz cousins

speak with common tongue and purpose / word is
sacred mystically birthed from the source of creation so why we tryin to hurt it / i heard it
reverberates sound / expands universe eternal / developed in ecstatic flows off freestyle
no rehearsal / bring reversal
                        to unjust orders / paradigms of thought
we are more than what we bought / speak with the force for which our ancestors fought
sing songs of radical equality / beyond distinctions of race / religion / psychology
basic necessities shouldn't be an american monopoly / where is our apology
lyrically follow me / dig me
                        like archeology
struggle with persistence to shed light on colonial realities
this instance
                i build strength like popeye
                cuz i eats me spinach / weak rappers / like sunsets
                when darkness come they diminish
                i shine / this is a race for your mind
                there is no finish
                line / we are beyond time

                        in a cipher
                        there is no mine
                        distinction is blind

oral hygiene

there will be no more
sweet talk: we are fucked up
and all my teeth are rotting

Post No Bills

1

teacher said

don't write on walls
stay between the lines

Moors slit scribes wrists
let no Hebrew script inside

english run rabid thru dark lands
leaving tongues of mother tied

pharaoh whipped the hieroglyphs
enslaved the pyramids rise

it was illegal for a black man to write
it was illegal for a black man to write

and mayor koch invested millions
to keep Puerto Ricans from bombing New York
but billions kept America bombing Vieques

and mayor daley classifies graffiti as mob action
but his father made a machine out of mob bosses

i'm no graff apologist
the empire has been bombing
long before kids accessed aerosol

bombing propaganda uncle sam in WWI
bombing blocks with poppy seeds, crack rocks and guns
     NRA registered glocks pointed at black cats by black cops
     shooting your own skin tone while klansmen sit back and watch
bombing our minds with bleach
bombing children before they speak
     what will the meek inherit
     we too busy chasin carrots
     9-5, forty plus hours a week
     my pops is comin home beat
     to collapse with a Pabst in his seat

before the television to beat himself
till battered vision deletes the chasm
between have and wishin
he beatin self for facts and fictions
beatin self like flagellant christians
be beating eardrums with hymnals
for false gods

they said religion
wd be separate from the state
but the state has become our dog
the pew is the market place, the pastor a wolf
hunting sheep to mow the fields
a blue-eyed white-collar armani suit
the devil's got mass appeal
he stashin deals with cash concealed
stealing lands and magic fields
cuffin hands of black skins
sendin bounty hunters to spirit kill

    till the white man stands atop the land screaming from the hill
    i own the earth on which you stand and you can **P**ost **N**o **B**ills

    till the white man stands atop the land screaming from the hill
    i own the earth on which you stand and you can **P**ost **N**o **B**ills

2

all Diaspora people
    come Now
your children swinging
latchkeys like slingshots
gather in encampments
around the writer's bloc

our language too subtle
a verbal capoeira beneath the radar
screen of dominant linguistics
we speak in tongues

hands full of phat caps and krylon cans
black books tucked in back pockets
we are the same new skool clandestine mystics
scribbling imagination on freight trains
bus seats, stop signs and brown lines
in journals and classrooms we wreck
magical havoc on open mics like Christ
in front of Lazarus weeping
bubble letters and wild-styles
crying our culture back to life

you've seen us
in your freedom dreams
at mid-night marauding
beneath the fallen stars
of broken lamp lights
Posting New Beliefs

ancient scribes
scrawling secret codes like:
Phresh **N**u **B**ombings
Postapocalypse **N**ow **B**egininng
Pigs **N**eed **B**ackup
Proletariats **N**ever **B**ackdown
Protecting **N**ubians & **B**oriquas
a call to headz everywhere:
Please **N**ow **B**ecome
Please **N**ow **B**ecome
Please **N**ow **B**e   a Nation

letters before buffing

heB-boy poetica: travel/in man

before the transfer raised a quarter
i'd be out my door   w/ a $1.80
thru turnstiles / mind wild / flippin pages to safety
my notebook on the L train / make headz flame like propane
Chicago pressed to pen n pad like Miles sketched Spain
choreographed the Windy / writing freely / a baggy pants Carl Sandburg
recordin life in 3D   what's beneath me /
                             placed upon this parchment
                             millions of shadows beneath industrial apartments
                             spark sessions to talk shit with mass transit commuters
                             use to blues change now white collar computers
choose the same routes
my father once chose to travel
buses, trains thru red line pain babble
earth crumblin like gravel / kids sentenced to life
underneath a judge's gavel
                                    i battle for sanity sometimes fallin off like saddle
                                    i'm mad at this century that is steerin us like cattle
                                    into deeper divides our lives perpetually is fragile
                                    speakin in one tongue we continuously babble-
on disaster
                     cover Self in workmen's plaster
                     now i spit class matters / unite rappers
                     till segregated streets signs / get ghost like Casper
                         compute the data / workers whisper in wind
                         my grandfather's arthritic hand speak thru my pen
                                 tracin generations
          runnin from Russian shtetls to Mississippi migration
                  heart racin
from the West Side to Uptown
big shoulders beaten down
at the daley press conference we meetin clowns
bozos and zeros / where Emma Goldman all my heroes
Harold Washington poisoned by peers so it seems
Fred Hampton got shot speakin truth to the machine
they prettying the streets but it's the mind that should be clean
they prettying the streets but it's the mind that should be clean
they prettying the streets
                                    but it's the mind

disconnect: 1984 & the failure of education or CPS gets an F   U

what you readin, joe

                this book sucks, dog

two boys banter on the orange line west
vocational high school english teachers assigned Orwell's classic

              i gotta write about this dude bein watched

for real?

salesmen head back to new england via Midway
hold laptop leather bags closer on creased khakis

the boys exit at Pulaski
55 yrs after the book first dropped

what you gonna write about

              i don't even know

blue light box video recorders hover
over street lamp corners like spaceships

aliens in the hood
big brother in blue

is white, always
watching

shorty talk shit

like he an old skool vet
blacxploytation pimp, rap don

shorty talkin all types of shit
draggin his lil azz to school (or not)

talkin bout bitches and rims
rides he's eight years early for

blunts, con-g-ac, girls he's run up in
his dreams are still droughts, doubts

all types of ill shit sleeps in his eyes
swoll thugd hard headz on the radio

around his neck like Flav did time
shorty a tickin clock of apocalypse

jappin on the mansions he don't got
places he won't go, he know names

of gated worlds he'll never enter
all grown up, shorty talkin mad

RAZOR RAMON'S

he cuts hair
at Luquillio's
on Division
between metal
flags, red&blue
sirens dancing
over the street

sharp with a blade,
straight edges circle
my mouth, his hands
clean, close cropped
finger nails like fades
he gives, tight, fresh 1
and 1/2 on top, sides
bald, baby powder
dusts ears done

Ramon is an Aries
all weekend long
he'll turn 22, friday
mambo, saturday
hip-hop at Slick's
sunday his moms
cooks bacolao, cousins
dress in white like
the *tres leches* cake
with his name on it

Ramon been waitin
                    on his case
                    4 years, armed
                    robbery cd catch
                    him 6, says he'll
                    serve 2 and 1/2
for good behavior

when he gets out
he wants to open
a barber shop, hopes
Omar lets him back
to pass out flyers

he sez
it'll be real nice
w/ good music, a spot
yous chill in, kinda
like a community center
n above de outside
the sign gonna say

ethnic cleansing

1

last night a 15-year-old father turned swiss cheese
last breath left his body like lobsters in boiling tombs

animal Crackers assumed his identity
shot premature ejaculates into the shadows
of ghost children hung before trial

this mourning abortion cries sun over the make-shift / memorial
arranged before gutted sidewalks of lego mansions
where the boy's body was found

mothers, nurses, homies, sisters, preachers, drug dealers
leave loose-leaf paper prayers, teddy bears, candles, white castles
his graff crew's black book, a photo album flipped open
pictures of the virgin mary and a young man in church
playing christ on good friday / back strained beneath the cross

2

day one/ poetry workshop / Wells High School / Javier cussed me out
in front of the whole class sayin i didn't know shit bout bein Puerto Rican from the hood *nada*
true / no doubt / next day brought in Willie Perdomo's *Where I'm From* / told students / write
your own shit / where you at / and don't be bitin Will's style or mimicking gangsta thug fantasies
i mean i wanna hear your story

and Javier stuck a pen thru his arm / tapped the blood beauty he'd written
in spanglish and struggled while reading not to cry or kill or throw himself
out the fourth floor window of our classroom

after the session i asked if he wrote a lot / said he wrecked walls and freight trains
in the hours most people sleep or sex / when boyfriends beat young mothers
of younger children who steal spray cans / and bomb rail yards and yuppie condos
along blue lines of Chicago L-trains / said

i'm tryin to make shit real pretty / like make bricks come alive with colors and
cartoon characters / positive messages like crack is for plumbers / toys are x-mas gifts
knowhutimsayin / make shit cold like Chi winters / mad flame like Chi summers / i mean
i wanna see people seein my shit / you know / jus see 'em seein my art / i mean
i jus want people to see how beautiful my shit is

3

a black sedan hides the immaculate on Wood Street
searching like pioneers for the perfect raw untapped fix-me-up

white collars won't step into the street this month
too many *chulos* on the porch packing rattraps and garden tools
selling *limonada* and furniture / there is no spring in this city
only gray and unbearable heat

two days from Javier's murder
estates will be spotless / memory expunged
streets and sanitation will wash the remnants
of a boy's life into an underground sepulcher

across the street
nieces and nephews watch police pick at crime scenes
architects pick up blueprints / new mothers pick wallpaper
patterns / the children pick out pages in history books / draw
mustaches on Mount Rushmore / to see if the stone heads
resemble the stone men / moving into the homes
they've been bought out of

for only another moment will these sounds   hang

                                          in the air
like bubble letters on buildings before buffing
like aerosol beneath moonbeams just after spray

the sound of boys kicking a *fútbol*
pebbles crunching under their feet
their sisters giggling at the mess they've made
of peeled mangos and limes / sweet juices and rind
sweating down their faces / seeping into the concrete
like blood

boomerang

54 minutes ago
they were searched by in-school security
for being high school students
one day after Colorado

> *why they gotta search us*
> *we didn't do anything*

class begins with the Tribune's headline
Maybe Now America Will Wake Up

the president says
and they don't know what he means
because the violence because the violence because the violence which has shocked
a privileged blind sector of the population controlled their movement since conception

they've already woken up
at night to the **CLACK CLACK** buckshot
not knowing who / this time 15 suburban folks
arrived to death sooner than they nightmared

> *it's just how it is, it's like the other day*
> *my cousin got run up on and shot 3 times*
> *but janet reno's psychologists aren't comin*
> *to hear my trauma, knowhutimsayin?*

here they wake up to **CLACK CLACK** terror jackhammering gentrification
making family homes mobile / pounding job loss and tax hikes
until white dog owners move in

> *ay yo, kev*
> *lemme ax a question, man*
> *this is one thing they can't blame on rap music*
> *i mean Tupac didn't kill in colorado*
> *no colored man killed in colorado*
> *so who they gonna blame*

and every radio mouth runs to blabber committee hearings
harvard professors of education / retired Lt. Col's emerge
from think tank utopian vacuums to scream esteemed opinions

...and for more on the story let's go to the scene of the slaughter

uh, yes Peter, i'm here with young/scared/hero/victim
he's wearing camouflauge cargo pants and an old navy bomber jacket
now son, what have you gained from this experience...

senators and religious fundamentalists roll up dollars and arms
lick their chops to graffiti HATE on ungodly systems they evangelized

this world bought for you by missionary corporations
who encourage you to spend more time in front of their altar

-nating

NATO bombs
dropping
out of advertisements we work for
while tough talk shit hosts kick suffering around   like foreign labor

how do you express your anger

i asked Latino students in room 222
and lazy 2nd period english class
they answered

just chill
hang with my girl
smoke herb

and i tried talkin expression
bout how you allow angst to manifest without bullets
like emcees spittin lyrics killin wack wordsmyths in freestyle ciphers but
they weren't hearin me
cuz 54 minutes ago
they were accused of being
the killers they have always been
accused of being

CLACK CLACK CLACK CLACK

when Malcolm X was asked about the assassination of JFK his calm wisdom dictated
the metaphysics of violence thru agricultural parables, he said a farmer lets chickens out
in the morning and at night is always glad to see them return, so when asked if he felt sorrow

for the american president being shot in front of his own country, he said he was always glad
to see chickens come home to roost

CLACK CLACK

i hope the president meant wake up like zen master
slapping wooden stick on back of america
enlightening us now / (but i know he didn't)

CLACK CLACK

we are looking at ourselves in the mirror
wondering   / when we got so ugly

CLACK CLACK

Charlton Heston didn't read the script carefully
in that Bible   / movie /   he acted in

CLACK
               we can't duck
from the boomerang
once thrown it speeds up
develops new technology
comes back to murder / the inventor

        so who we gonna blame

day dreams
after William Stafford

1

i am a poet
on television commercials
composing jingoist jingles
for public consumption
my words common
as a hallmark card
and war reports
on the ten o'clock news

2

i am a poet
drunk in a puddle
of worry where next word
will emerge from, the muse
bitter from suicide notes
swallowed with old style
and old milk chasing death's tail
with a shot glass full of women

3

i am a poet
armwrestling language
in tweed straitjackets
with a distinguished panel
of dialogical idolaters
praying a department head
chair will be shoved
up my ass

4

i am a poet
rockin hot spots
mic jockin my pole
position spittin word
glisten in ya girl's
ignition wishin
upon i wish
i were a star

5

i am a poet
ex-patriot plotting a return
to the scene, though not ready
are they for my (re) turn
re: turn   are they?
red e   eeeeeeeeeeee!!!!!!
for wire-rimmed me/my me/my
movement: angstangstangst

6

i am a poet
monk, breathe
morning words
before sunrise i
exhale visions
supplicated
in front of the altar
of blank pages

7

i am a poet
on tour with product
and groupies rock
& roll high off poems
written four years ago
in my parent's basement
when i was hungry

8

i am a poet
in Chicago
capturing words
in notebooks
snapshots of a people
working i am
crafting the world
around me as it is

mettLe respires

silence is pending

a din
    suspended

        between rounds
        a death rattle caught
        in the lungs / a pigeon
        orchestra tuning in the cage
            of beige bones

shadows box on Wabash / black
ten
    dons
        hang
            like
                ropes

and it comes

the roar of drums / ten thousand
marching / a pendulum speeding
through the body / breath's pugilism
the champ's cry rocking iron / thunder
rumbles to a standstill
                    steel gaspssssss
      hawk claws over metal
      screeeeeeeeeeeeechhh

      workers empty train lines
      mister charlie don't ride
      his office / children / bed linens
      clean at the Palmer House

Frank and Philip's barbershop
newsstands / proprietor stools
franchised delis / cup clinkers
collect change

                              disdain
                    drops

futures determined here
traded with pork bellies

orange vested surgeons
dance the high-wire act

Metropolitan Correctional inmates hear
economic shifts wheel through window slits

the round resumes

dreams stalk beneath the canopy of tremble
multitudes rush routed in the iron Lasso
and from time to time
          we all
          look
          up
          awed
          crook-
          necked
          amazed this old
          fighter won't fall

love letter to chi

i have loved you since i first stood
at your North Shore borders patroled
with suburban whispers of disimagination

i gazed longingly
at the transit tunnels you bore
like river channels, tentacles
reaching into lily white
flight pad picket fences
where jews sold themselves
for the price of a nose job

i fell in love with you
on school field trips
head out bus window
staring at invisible neighborhood lines
that decree where the world's refugees will sleep

i see them scattered thru Wicker Park
Little Village and Pilsen
spanish knotted in their tongues
generations of families
the orkin man is trying to genocide

in Albany park
i've eaten in the Mexican bakeries
open to the masses marching towards transit loops
samsara CTA lines dumping lives in nine-hour cubicles
downtown where the rich live and oversee the poor
people dwindling in the shadows of skyscrapers

i've heard meringue dance in bungalow alleys
at 2 am
car horns are doorbells four hours later
metallic roosters that call Korean shop owners
to open laundromats to globe traveled women
who wash with futility, the stench of kim chi
bacoloa, cumin, turmeric, gefilta fish and chitterlings

this what you smell like on a good day
on Division or Devon, 75th and Indiana
18th west of Ashland before the blue line
that doesn't run on the weekends
grilled elotes, the pinch of cayenne
in your nose

my father loves you cuz of the kosher hot dogs
at Wrigley Field, he skipped school in 1953
when Ernie Banks came up from the Kansas City
Monarchs for the last 13 games of season
and Nate, who worked in his father's print shop
told him that once the cubs get a black ballplayer
they'd win the pennant and, though mathematically
impossible,my father believed and went and waits
till next year like Ernie who played 19 seasons
confined in the in not-so-friendly confines of green ivy
waiting on next year for the promise like the Pullman Porters
and domestic workers and pig slaughterers and daughters
of Mississippi field hands who wait on reparations

i mean the cubs deserve a pennant like your black metropolis
deserves paycheck and payback and institutions built in their name
run by the children
whose fathers you murdered while sleeping in their own beds
whose food you poisoned during a luncheon meeting at city hall
who you shot for trying to organize tortilla workers
for swimming on your beaches
or playing in your Marquette Parks

i love you despite your cook county holding cells
the glass precipice of your juvenile detention centers
glaring violet, red sunsets over the domes of the kidnapped

i love you despite your insistence on tracking and standardized tests
despite your area 21 plan
fuck you for lincoln park and university village

i love you because i know a Haymarket riot eats at your innards

i love you
for the farm boys you pulled beneath lamplights
for the Louisiana white girl Gwendolyn Brooks called here
for the Asian women whose hands dry clean your white collars
and their children born with two tongues spitting pins out their mouths

i have loved you since hoping the Skokie swift
and transferred to the red line then to the blue line
and then to Maxwell Street to get fitted for my first X cap

i have loved you since Lit-X spoke Africa and Oshun in my ear
i love you cuz of the young authors
stock piling notebooks in their bedrooms
roaming the streets with pen and paper tucked under one arm
in their backpacks right now, writing, recording the everyday
moments of everyday people, resisting your graffiti blaster white wash
your gentrified dystopias, your monotoned broken stringed blues halls

Chicago
Studs Terkel is still recording
your parks are bigger than before
       like your poor and workless
thousands ready to wrestle for your affection
i hope you let those who love the whole of you
those who have felt the tight grip of your taxes
those who ride the CTA, the fruit packers
who stand at North and Western from 5 am waiting labor
who round children and grandchildren in west-side bunk beds
who concoct schemes to stay in your boarders with carts of mangos
paleta pushers, dog walkers, security officers, mechanics, street
pharmacologists, L-train musicians, swindlers, kids with M&Ms
trying to afford basketball uniforms, Sun-Times rush hour salesmen
lower Wacker homeowners, 3 card monte-hide-a-nut red line entertainers
teaching-poets, graf artists and all folks on the hustle
i hope you continue to be a source of frustration and love
a lakeside tree shielding sun, a south shore BBQ
a place we can live and not be squeezed out like mustard
pickle, relish and tomato when you hold on to your hotdog
too tightly

slingshots

return train from Indiana

i want to write quiet poems about lone conductors
pushing South Shore lines through Michigan City
after midnight, sounding whistles that ricochet ghost
echoes off discarded factories from Hammond to Calumet

i want to write about the family of birds
who gather at Aunt Roz's window before sunrise
insisting she wake after restless nights of drinking alone
in her second floor efficiency, son Jerry chose not to return, she thinks
birds whisper his name so angels will write it in the book of eternity

i'd even write how my mom looks before sleep
a little girl in pajamas smiling like she has secrets
gossip, tales of boys who crushed her, face scrubbed
raw and paintless, a beautiful stranger whose eyes dream
in Roz's living room, our slumber party on chez lounges

i'd write family myths, mundane ice cream cones
incorporate greek g-ds into everyday triviality, invent forms
get an mfa, read Lowell, chuckle with Billy Collins over parsnips
overcoats draped over one arm walking over the campus in sweaters

hai coup

assimilation
jams pig meat in our throats
offers cash on our altars

underground chi-town battle rap for a dying zionist

old man you jock republicans like barnacles
regeanomic nut sacks packed in your mouth
like clowns by the carloads / i hope your heart holds
more space than trucks in united parcel / you sold the star
skyward to the highest goliath barcode / Hashem's sparks froze
now King David throws rocks with slingshots from the golan heights
of idols / resurrect fly kikes like Arhendt and Goldman round the riot pole
we suppose those chose rock sandals and halos / but you arm guard the ark
with handguns and frayed souls / i'm afraid those / gates closed on Moses's
five books / won't be opend by idiot boxing rabbis posing grateful as paid rooks
don't we find it odd the evangelical is our bedfellow / we wallow in tastey pig cakes
claimin we never had trouble / but best believe when i see jerry falwell on tv / i guess what
he's thinkin / *give money to satan's children til our lord comes back to beseech them* / 144,000
doesn't mean you Jew / we lost in the house of babble backing the fork tongued and feeble
minded lairs / hypocrite Holocaust deniers

> the middle east is an oil field, Israel could be set on fire
> as long as corporate shields protect the saved thru muck and mire

> the middle east is an oil field, Israel could be set on fire
> as long as corporate shields protect the saved

no better

we know better
have known bitter
each year marror
matzah sandwiches of affliction
parsley slave tears / late night exodus
we fled all of europe / first blamed
hid secrets in our shoes / diaspora
culture where we populate / infiltrate
assimilate / the world's finest chameleons
we could look light / white / like hosts
walk into diners after sunsets and order bacon
new names to pass / knew the new deal / the seal
tucked between legs trembling before shiksa infidelities

we were nervous Woody Allen / delirious Lenny Bruce / our fridays were different
Aunt Tessie / raisin kugel / poor athletes became bookies / loose ties to the mob
minstrel Al Jolsons / quiet in secluded ghettos / Yiddish theater / wide-hipped women
calling Brooklyn boys from stick ball / west side Chicago alleys

before we owned and exploited / when we were kikes / before we stopped mimicking
black resistance / began rushing pinstripes past mezuhzaed framed doors / shaved beards
reformed synagogues with church hymnals / collection plates / no longer a community center
houses of gossip and rhinoplasty / before we could pass

we know better / been sold / burned into soap / butter / said never again
wrote hope letters / heeded words of prophets / post-holocaust ghost men
we diamond merchants for profit / i'd rather keep wandering / if this the price
to build a nation / what we gonna teach our children / police work assassination
our past is waitin for reclamation / we Sabbath agents testin Hashem's patience

before '67 wars were biblical / mythical / spiritual
no army of the littered / no monster truck fleets of bulldozers
no blood on our hands / finger prints staining borrowed triggers
we were Eisteinian pacifists / Marxian labor leaders / folk dancers
like Goldman / we stood on moral ground

in babylon we've become xenophobes
revisionist historians / pig eaters / baby killers
erectors of walls / border guard republicans
mercenaries in jerry fallwell's war / idolaters
of christian economic science / we kneel before

investment bank junk bond insecurity brokers
sew resistant lips shut with strings of bullets
replace kibbutzim with Cowboy colonialists
rocketlaunch cooperatives / we have become

no better
                      than roman emperors
                            crusade leaders
                                  knesset klansmen
no better
                      than sharonian war criminals
                            arafatian castro infidels
                                  imperial ghetto kings
no better
                      than rabid hand puppets
                            golden calf slumlords
                                  genocidal amnesiacs

no better   than christians
no better   than white men
                   than neuvo fascists
                   than a million mccarthyites
no better   than syrian armies
                   than suicide bombers
                   than arab holocaust deniers
no better   than blind shepards
no better   than cain

we may know better
than all the world's sufferers
but are no better because of it

six million

murdered in Holocaust
we displace same # of
Palestinians

Hero Israel

the star belongs to no one, not David
would believe his child has become Goliath
spitting imperialist warheads at children
holding slingshots

if you are to be perfection
we must teach ourselves lessons missed assimilating
bacon breakfasts under the christmas tree
cleavers cutting bumps off our hooked noses
driving roman chariots on the Sabbath to execute
eviction notices in ghettos we once were wrangled in, too

Israel
you are the messenger
sent to gather ye children
of meta-tongue and supplication

have you lost your way

hunting salvation like lynch mob
in *traife* corners of anglo lands
you whore yourself to sleep in the hands of men
who will beat you after morning coffee

Israel
you   pawn
middle east western military base
you are strategic oil insurance
for american mongrels
who cut language from our lips with english-
named conversions like *Coval*,
who re-stitched circumcisions
mohels made with television wire,
who put bread and prosperity
before our famished mouths
we gnaw the covenant till it breaks centuries of Rivka's teachings
we worship the emperor's idols like they were our G-d's
we wonder diaspora dead

Israel where is Judith to chop off your head
what have you done with Rabbi Nachman

can you alone be chosen
in an interconnected universe
will you open your doors to all children
who cry silent in bombed nights

Jerusalem and Ramallah
The West Bank and Gaza

your daughters wandered forty years
seeking a place to rest their family, praise existence
birth future messiahs who will bring forth *baruch*
words in ears of G-d's millioned mouths

will you listen Israel
for the messenger calls constant,
before which altar do you burn incense

i saw you in South Africa
quiet in the back room
Steve Biko's holy hands were murdered

in Liberia your diamonds drip dead
fingerprints, fund limousines for the *rebbe*
to view memorial cheesecake tourist factories
in Tel Aviv city centers

i can no longer witness
Israel i can no longer bear to witness
thousands of murdered Palestinian children
dragged onto the empty box that stares
into my screams and say i can't see
what you are doing, i see you, Israel
i see you

and yes, i saw you
in Crown Heights murdered by half brothers
walking on egg shells since destruction of the first temple
and yes   i think they might come for us again
and yes   i imagine Gestapo in new uniforms
                    Austrian, German or Confederate

and yes   i am scared to wear my *yarmulke* in public
i don't want numbers burned into my skin
or be asked to show my horns

i am paranoid with historical precedence

but i am not myself
Israel who are you

your message is cryptic
and i can't read Hebrew

shema yisrael adonai eloheinu adonai echad[1]

Hear O Israel, the Lord *is* One,
so when will you stop killing

                        yourself

- -

1 *most commonly recited Hebrew prayer,* Here O'Israel, The Lord our G-d, The Lord is One

Ibrahimi Mosque or Cave of the Patriarchs

Jews and Muslims
spit on Abraham's tomb
the same fucking tomb
it's
        the same

Yosef's Reveries

1

when i saw
an old woman
on all fours
in the ruins
of her home
looking under
floor tiles
for medicine
i did think
what would i say
if it were my grandmother

2

we must bring whiteout home from the office
and paint our eyes while watching tv, we are

killing semites, notice; pronounced noses, skin
like olive pressed oils, bearded men hawking

sore syllables from the back of their thick throat,
the first palestinian i met could've been my sister

eyes like dates, lips full of sun, born in a refugee camp
her family pushed out cuz of passports and holy books

3

tell me you can't hear the echoes
tell me your eyes are too sore from tears
            and squinting to see the similarities
tell me we have not become oil hound slumlords
tell me we are not Jews but school of the americas dropouts
tell me we have not crossed this side of history
welcomed the stranger at nervous triggered checkpoints

where is her bed of hay
plate of figs, tepid water
to bathe in

qadosh

we are poets each / of us travelers between / history and hope
~Suheir Hammad

1

everything
     as i
     as u
     as all

2

on the earth
      snow
covered minnesota

you opened
Creation/
      (')s
hidden mirror

peek-a-booed
paradigms / mystics
hunt for ages

reflections we are
never ready to gaze in

3

i too wd like to count
infinity in one sitting

4

at seven
death was a curse
sermoned by bully pulpit rabbis
and poster children for the Nuclear family

i hid at night
beneath Star Wars
bed sheets shaking
at the promise of being
forgotten

5

at nineteen
i ate mushrooms, strawberries
melt my hand in Lake Michigan
where sky and water gather
at the horizon and blues
brush and smog pink
graffiti streaks and sun
sets red and i knelt at the lips
of the Great body facing east
forehead lowered to sand-

malkut's majesty

6

before rebirth /
poems and pardons
at the altar

i believe in

        chance
        change
        chango
        chicago
        chippewa
        charlie chaplin
        challah
        cha cha cha...

to say we have met is true
and if we do again, bless/ed
and if we do not, bless/ed

for you are forever
with me like fingerprints,
which is more than i can say
for ashes floating down stream

7

qadosh!
qadosh! everything
lips eyes ass qadosh! breath qadosh!
long fingers small hands qadosh!
straight nappy full black ringlets qadosh!
stomach legs breasts qadosh! impermanence qadosh!
nothingness in our heads qadosh! heart stops time break beats qadosh!
fishermen and fish mortuaries qadosh! willow branches prostrating qadosh!
tied tongues wrung upon paper ghosts qadosh! immigrant diaspora qadosh!
all this wandering qadosh! mothers fathers prisoners qadosh! silent bookstore
histories qadosh! record bin archaeologies qadosh! June Jordan qadosh! Kris Parker qadosh!
Kool Herc qadosh! emptiness qadosh! form qadosh! all manifestations of non-duality qadosh!
symmetry chemistry poetry uncertainty qadosh! coming night qadosh! samsara suffering
qadosh! palestine qadosh! israel qadosh! a new jerusalem qadosh! sabbath bread breaking
qadosh! truth for my people qadosh! wrestling ancestral warfare qadosh! against time qadosh!
protest qadosh! rocks qadosh! no walls qadosh! here qadosh! together qadosh! now qadosh!
now qadosh!

8

i hope
we travel
near again

poets naming

all
          that is

when Ishmael comes home

his beard will be knotty
nappy hair wrapped in cloth
ain't no scissors in exile
no bathtubs or green lawns

his feet bandaged and blistered
fingertips calloused pulling bows
back to fling stone headed arrows
at bandits who try to steal on him

he shall be a wild ass of man
his hand against all, hand of all
against him[1]

wandering streets and alleys
hard rock on mug, grill chiseled
scrapping with crumb snatchers
who scurry for kingdom-issued cheese

> *cuz where i'm at, if your soft, you're lost*
> *to stay on course means to roam with force*
> *every day i see my mother Hagar strugglin*
> *now it's time i've got to do somethin*[2]

Hagar, slave woman of Abraham
forced to grow seed in Sara's barren field
and service fresh cut cock of the patriarch
Hagar, who waded in the water one night
fleeing for freedom called back by G-d's promise
that of her son *a nation I will make of him*[3]
and she always wanted to be queen
to preside over frivolous decisions
like which napkin set to serve the dignitaries
and watch her son grow in the soft surroundings of excess

but only bread and water
when banished into the wilderness of Be'er Sheva,
mother and son sinking in the Well of Seven Swearings
where curses and unmentionables
lay beneath African blood sand
and back alimony

Hagar cursed G-d with talmudic fervor one night
her son on the orphanage auction block of revisionist history
she demanded to know where is his angel tonight
where is the hand of compassion to unbind my son
from the bloody sheath of your affliction

when Ishmael comes home
he'll be called by half-brother Isaac
he'll duck stones and pagan rituals
through the desert he'll carry a cross
of questions for his father like
>   *why i banished from eternity's promise*
>   *why i whited-out stories told my brother*
>   *bout how my mother wuz no good woman*
>   *while drinking grapes in the temple*
>   *did you pour some out to remember me*
>   *for the covenant i am a testament*
>   *to your cowardice, 613 tsi-tsi knots strung*
>   *around my neck hung wonderin who i wuz*
>   *cuz you cut family ties*

when Ishmael comes home
he will speak pidgined hebonics
tongue tied in the tastes of hummus
brown olives and women
he could haggle in the philistine markets
saddle donkeys, slay ewes, play dominos
roll tobacco and hash in cigarette papers
drink wine in the brothelled ghettos of the east

he will pray fervently
five times toward Mecca
where seeds cast into wind
bloom prophets and civilizations
his face dark, weather-beaten skin
like sun at dusk, eyes blood shot
witness to women raped by outlaws
        and kings

when Ishmael comes home
the border patrol will stop him
he will be searched for bombs strapped to his chest
he looks too familiar, when asked to identify himself
he will show his scar, the skin seal his father stole from him
servants will whisper, old maids will remember
the boy's face like his father's cut at the chin
days of awe dreamed into the back of his eyes

he will walk through the doors and flowing curtains
past sculptures and bed frames, past ram horns
nephews, nieces and the ashes of broken idols
into a house of kin mourning, stand over the fallen
frame of his father, hand stretched holy warrior
he will grab his brother weeping and say

together we will dig this grave brother
lay the bones of a man I never knew
cover earth over him, say Kaddish
we will mourn together my brother
did he tell you my name, that I look like you
love you, dreamed to have a brother
at night sleeping curled under my lineage

my lord is Allah, is Yahweh, is what saved you
atop the mount and dammed me to wander
I am strong, brother, do not weep cuz the patriarch
is gone, death is rebirth is time to build new temples
tell stories of our father, sing his praises, mend his curses
stand over his memory and decide where to move from here

Isaac, I have returned
my shoes are off in your home
my open palm extends to you
Salaam, Shalom, in peace
brother, will you take my hand

----

1 *Genesis 15:12*
2 *Boogie Down Productions, "Love's Gonna Getcha" from the Edutainment album*
3 *Genesis 21:13*

SHOUT OUTS

there are going to be too many people to name, but this is hip-hop
& at the party everyone likes to hear their name thru the speakers so...

my family: moms, dad, e (i love you, i am so proud of the man you've become) elyse, mama (we oughta have some pancakes now), joyce, cheryl, arnie, stephen and nina, skylar and lily, chuck and lauren, adam (whut up cuz/ bro/ soon to be papa), julie, jill and amy, brit and kimmy, imissu papa (wanna to make some awangments)- bubbe pearl and zadie george, i meet you every time your children speak your name- all my aunts and cousins (way too many to name) i am honored to be down with y'all, good lookin and keep the kugel comin

my people: eboo patel, lisa arrastia, idris goodwin, shradha patel, anna west, leo, anton, rebecca (love patience time), krista franklin, avery r. young (in the place to be), pete kahn, mike hef, dove rock, mariah neuroth, dan sully, malika's kitchen, dennis kim, bone, bryonn bain and jason carne (i am grateful we buildin like that), kelly tsai, ugochi, rosa, umnia, tim stafford, kip kline, adam wienstock, qurash ali lansana, tara betts, gary lilley, xulan and aviatrix, josh macphee, roger bonair-agard, lynn procoe, marty mcconnell, bar 13 massive, mental graffiti, lucy anderton and nick fox, mr. itch 13 (we always gonna work together), cool out and amina, justin mayer, sonofwon, butta, ira and jon @ leo burrnet, the diatribe crew, casper, kane, dynamic vibrations, kamilah forbes and stan lathan, seemore perspective, adam mansbach, jeff chang, ben and biz 3, hermit arts, young chicago authors, kuumba lynx, lisa lee, kurt heinz, greg polvere and global talent, tanya and coya paz, fausto and apollo project, b-boy b and fly paper, cap d, mario and tina howell, j.love, emily evans and naïveté studios (this even looks like a book, damn)

my students/the future(now): before y'all start with *whatchu mean student, kevin / we not even in a classroom* - i just want to say i learn from y'all and you my people but we got a different thing goin, too- that's why i ask so many questions, so... mike booker, kevin derrig, lamon manuel, amanda torres, kristiana colon, alanna zaritz, lauren woods, we og crew- word up, matt ewing, sharif, santana, dorothea, noel, luis, allister, and all the college and high school students i meet on the road, thank you for sharing with me, the hidden and scribbled pages

many many thanks to the early readers of this manuscript: willie perdomo (i tell people you're my big brother), suheir hammad (we got much work to do, girl), mark nowak (afrika bam of the page), julie parson-nesbitt (what up, lil david)- (y'all my people too, but i wanted to give a little xtra luv)

my mentors and people who look out in general: bill ayers (you lead by example), brother wayne teasdale (who wdn't rest in peace, but tells jokes to all beings in consciousness), sylvia ewing (you care about young people cuz you still one), dr. charles strain, krs-one (rap needed a teacher and you became it), marc smith, rick benjamin, bob boone, michael warr, oba maja

finally to mark and ron @ em press: i'm not sure if this was a book when i brought it to you / ron, thank you for curving and pulling and cutting and long hours to make this a concise narrative and a whole piece- and mark, thank you for believing in me from the get, ever since spoken word revolution, thank you both for going thru this process with me, for all my phone calls, emails and general neuroses / thank you for opening up your homes and schools and lives and committing them to new poetics, scholars and gentlemen, i am lucky and grateful to be working with you

thank you whose hands and eyes rest and wrestle with these words
thank you for deciphering, for ciphering, for throwing down loot or coming to the show
thank you hip-hop, i still (used to) love you, you gave me a way to live

word/life - shalom/salaam

photo by Alanna Zaritz

KEVIN COVAL's writing has appeared in The Spoken Word Revolution (Sourcebooks Publishing), Awakening The Spirit (Skylight Paths), XCP: Cross-Cultural Poetics, Chicago Tribune, Chicago Reporter, Cross Currents, Crab Orchard Review, Garland Court Review, The Daily Herald, The Courier News, Fly Paper, seen on C-Span, four seasons of Russell Simmons HBO Def Poetry Jam and can be heard regularly on Chicago Public Radio.

Co-founder of The Chicago Teen Poetry Festival: Louder Than A Bomb, Coval serves as the Artistic Director of Young Chicago Authors. *Slingshots (A Hip-Hop Poetica)*, is his first book.

1. **elegy for Lit X**
~ *beat by Cool Out [www.urbanizedmusic.com]*
~ *from New Skool Poetics, Vol 1 [www.naiveterecords.com]*

2. **pieces of shalom**
~ *recorded by Butta, live @ Hot House*

3. **what moms had to do for a michael jordan autographed shoe**
~ *recorded by Butta, live @ Urban Sandbox*

4. **white boy ballad for a southern b-girl**
~ *recorded by Jon Sieller @ Jon Doe Studios*

5. **nothing fight (a battle cry)**
~ *recorded by Justin J. Mayer @ Boom!*

6. **Post No Bills**
~ *beat by sonofwon*

7. **The Day Jam Master Jay Died**
~ *recorded by Jon Sieller @ Jon Doe Studios*

8. **RAZOR RAMON'S**
~ *from WBEZ's 848, 91.5 fm, Chicago Public Radio*

9. **boomerang**
~ *recorded live @ Amherst College*

10. **love letter to chi**
~ *beat by Cool Out [www.urbanizedmusic.com]*

11. **Hero Israel**
~ *recorded by Justin J. Mayer @ Boom!*

12. **qadosh**
~ *recorded by Justin J. Mayer @ Boom!*

- - - - - - - - - - - - - - - - - - - -
mastered by Justin J. Mayer